Where Did I

WAYLAND

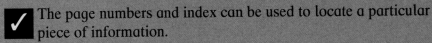

All Wayland books encourage children to read and help them improve their literacy.

✓ The page numbers and index can be used to locate a particular piece of information.

✓ The glossary reinforces alphabetic knowledge and extends vocabulary.

✓ The books to read section suggests other books dealing with the same subject.

First published in 1998 by
Wayland Publishers Ltd
This edition revised in 2007 by Wayland,
an imprint of Hachette Children's Books

British Library Cataloguing in Publication Data
Llewellyn, Claire,
Where did I come from?: a first look at sex education. – (Me and My Body)
1. Sex instruction   2. Juvenile literature
I Title II. Gordon, Mike 1948 –
649.6'5

ISBN 978 0 7502 5274 4

Printed and bound in China

Hachette Children's Books
338 Euston Road
London, NW1 3BH

ME AND MY BODY series:
Am I Fit and Healthy?
LEARNING ABOUT DIET AND EXERCISE

Nice or Nasty?
LEARNING ABOUT DRUGS AND YOUR HEALTH

Where Did I Come From?
A FIRST LOOK AT SEX EDUCATION

Why Wash?
LEARNING ABOUT PERSONAL HYGIENE

Where Did I Come From?

A FIRST LOOK AT SEX EDUCATION

Written by Claire Llewellyn
and
illustrated by Mike Gordon

Some of us aren't sure where we came from.

We don't know how we began.

Who should we ask?

Your mum or dad know all about you.

They knew you before you were born.

Where you came from is one of their favourite stories. Why not ask them to tell it to you?

Your mum and dad met
a long time ago.
They got to know each
other better ...

... and better.

They loved one another so much that
they decided to make a home together.

After a while, they wanted to have a baby.
They wanted to have **you**.

Your mum and dad can make a baby because their bodies are different.

Your mum's body contains eggs and your dad's body contains tiny seeds called sperm.

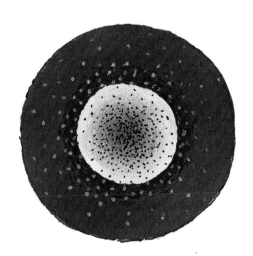

egg from mum

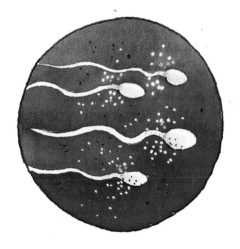

sperm from dad

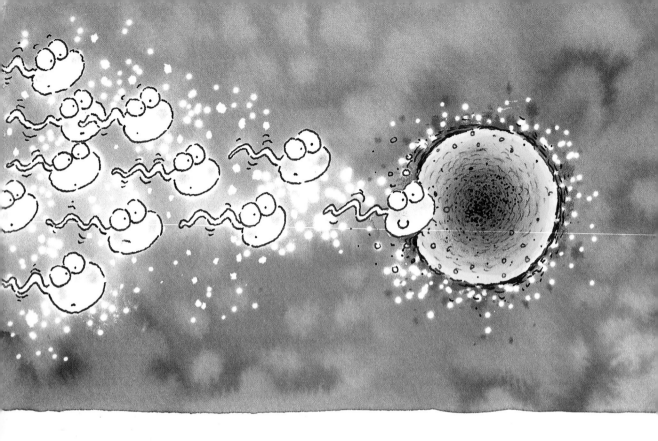

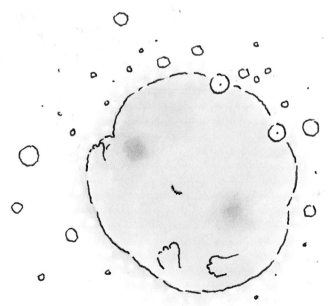

Mum and dad can join their bodies together. When a sperm from dad meets an egg from mum, it may start to grow into a baby.

This is how you began to grow, in your mum's body.

You grew safely inside your mum's body.
Over nine months you grew very fast
indeed. As you grew bigger, your mum
did too!

Your mum had a check at the hospital to make sure you were both well.

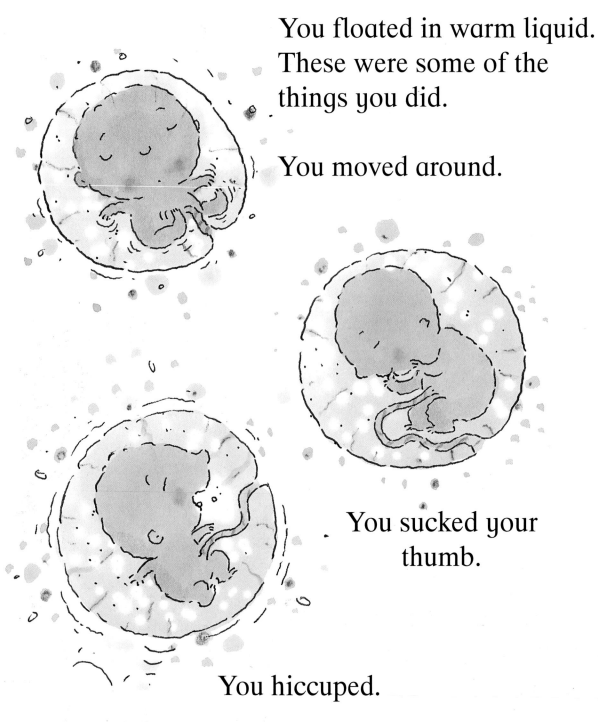

You floated in warm liquid.
These were some of the
things you did.

You moved around.

You sucked your
thumb.

You hiccuped.

You didn't have to eat or breathe for yourself because your mum did these things for you.

The two of you were joined together by a cord that gave you food and oxygen.

The cord was where your tummy button is today.

It takes nine months for a baby to grow.
During that time, your mum and dad got
everything ready for you.

They may have painted your bedroom,
and bought you all the things a new
baby needs.

At long last you were ready to be born.
You were pushed out of your mum's
body. It was hard work.

Your mum and dad saw you for the very first time. They cuddled you and talked to you.

They loved you from the moment you were born.

Caring for a baby is a full-time job.

Your mum and dad fed you ...

changed you ...

comforted you ...

bathed you ...

dressed you ...

fed you ...

BURP

and comforted you some more ...

... all through the day and night.

Week by week, you grew bigger and stronger, and learned to do lots of new things.

In time, you began to feed yourself ...

dress yourself ...

and wash yourself.

25

When you were bigger, perhaps your mum
and dad had another baby – a sister or
brother who became part of your family.

When mum was busy or dad was tired, you could still go with a friend to the park.

You're not a baby any more, of course,
though you're growing and learning still.

Just think that, whatever our size, we all began just the same way. We once grew inside our mother's body out of a tiny egg.

TOPIC WEB

Maths
Find out who in the class has brothers and sisters, and how many. How many children are there in the biggest family? How many have no siblings? Record the results in a chart.

Design and Technology
Design and make a simple toy or cloth book for a young baby, making sure it is safe for a baby to put in its mouth.

History
Invite in some parents and grandparents to discuss how they cared for their babies to find out the similarities and differences.

Science
Draw pictures of a man and a woman, labelling the body parts, including the reproductive system. Discuss the foods that babies and small children need to enable them to grow.

Geography
Find out about family life in a different locality being studied. What kind of family set-ups are typical and how do they compare with those of the class?

Where Did I Come From?

R.E.
Find out about the ceremonies held by people of different religions to welcome new babies into the world.

Language
Talk about the feelings of an older child towards the new baby. Write a poem about the habits and activities of a new baby, using as many descriptive words as possible.

Art and Craft
Find photos in magazines and newspapers showing babies and families around the world and make a display.

Music
Make up a simple, repetitive song to teach a baby a simple set of words, for example, parts of the body. Add actions so the baby can understand and imitate.

P.E./Dance/Drama
Explore the movements that a baby can make before it can walk, for example, rolling, pulling the body along, crawling, moving on its back.

GLOSSARY

cord A tube that joins a mother and baby.

oxygen A gas that we need in our bodies to live.

sperm The seed in a male that can start new life.

tummy button Another name for the 'knot' on the tummy called the navel.

BOOKS TO READ

How are Babies Made? by Alistair Smith (Usborne, 1998)

How a baby forms inside its mother, including lift-up picture flaps which show growth and change.

How did I Begin? by Mick Manning and Brita Granstrom (Franklin Watts, 2004)

Simple explanations and answers to crucial questions about the facts of life.

Mummy Laid an Egg by Babette Cole (Red Fox, 2000)

The children put their parents right about the facts of life.

Our New Baby by Sarah Lavete (How do I Feel About? series, Franklin Watts, 1999)

How to cope with a new situation such as the birth of a younger brother or sister.

What About Me? by Pat Thomas (My Amazing Journey series, Wayland, 1999)

Picture book which explores the conception and birth of a child in simple terms.

The World is Full of Babies by Mick Manning and Brita Granstrom (Wonderwise series, Franklin Watts, 2004)

Looks at the growth and development of both humans and animals.

INDEX